HOLIDAY FUN

HOLI

KIM THOMPSON

NorwoodHouse Press

Cataloging-in-Publication Data

Names: Thompson, Kim.
Title: Holi / Kim Thompson.
Description: Buffalo, NY : Norwood House Press, 2027. | Series: Holiday fun | Includes glossary and index.
Identifiers: ISBN 9781978580657 (pbk.) | ISBN 9781978580664 (library bound) | ISBN 9781978580671 (ebook)
Subjects: LCSH: Holī (Hindu festival)--Juvenile literature.
Classification: LCC BL1239.82.H65 T548 2027 | DDC 394.261--dc23

Published in 2027 by
Norwood House Press
2544 Clinton Street
Buffalo, NY 14224

Designer: Rhea Magaro
Editor: Tricia Hoffman

Photo credits: Cover, p. 1 Kathriba/Shutterstock.com; pp. 5, 6, 21 Govind Jangir/Shutterstock.com; p. 7 ABHISHEK BASAK 90/Shutterstock.com; p. 8 Pete Niesen/Shutterstock.com; p. 9 pmraj2020/Shutterstock.com; p. 10 nelle hembry/Shutterstock.com; p. 12 Fotonium/Shutterstock.com; p. 13 Abu hasim asaru/Shutterstock.com; p. 15 Sumit Saraswat/Shutterstock.com; p. 16 Vyas Abhishek/Shutterstock.com; p. 18 Mikhail Klyoshev/Shutterstock.com; p. 19 Intellistudies/Shutterstock.com;

Printed in the United States of America

CPSIA compliance information: Batch #CSNHP27: For further information contact Norwood House Press at 1-800-237-9932.

TABLE OF CONTENTS

HOLI IS HERE!

Colors fly through the air. You get covered in green, orange, and purple.

On this **holiday**, it is fun to get messy. It is Holi (HOH-lee)!

A SPECIAL DAY

Holi comes every year. It is usually in March.

This **festival** celebrates the end of winter and the beginning of spring.

Holi is a special day for **Hindus**.

It began long ago in **India**.

Today, it is celebrated all over the world.

Holi is also called the festival of colors. On Holi, red **represents** love. Blue means peace. Green stands for new beginnings.

HOW TO CELEBRATE

To get ready for Holi, people make sweet **dumplings** called *gujiyas*.

They buy colored powders called *gulal*.

On the night before Holi, celebrations begin. People light **bonfires**. They sing and dance.

निकास मार्ग
केवल महिलाओं के लिये स्थान
केवल पुरुषों के लिये स्थान

In the morning, people put on old clothes. They go to **temples** and outdoor celebrations. They beat drums and dance.

People "play" Holi. This means they throw lots of *gulal*.

The powders can be mixed with water. Some people throw water balloons at each other!

On Holi, no one escapes getting showered with the bright colors of spring.

Everyone is messy and everyone is happy!

GLOSSARY

bonfires (BAHN-fires): large outdoor fires often made to celebrate special events

dumplings (DUHMP-lings): dough wrapped around fillings and boiled, fried, or steamed

festival (FES-tuh-vuhl): a celebration or holiday

Hindus (HIN-dooz): people who practice Hinduism, the religion of many people from India

holiday (HAH-li-day): a day when most people do not go to school or work because of a religious or national celebration

India (IN-dee-uh): a country in South Asia that has more people than any other country in the world

represents (rep-ri-ZENTS): stands for something else; acts as a sign or symbol

temples (TEM-puhls): religious buildings; places for practicing a religion and worshiping a god or gods

THINKING QUESTIONS

1. When is Holi?
2. Why do people wear old clothes on Holi?
3. Where did Holi begin?
4. Is music a part of Holi? How?
5. What is *gulal*? How do people use it on Holi?

INDEX

ABOUT THE AUTHOR

Kim Thompson lives in Columbus, Ohio, with her husband and two funny cats. She has written many books for kids. Her favorite color is green. Her favorite thing about spring is being able to ride her bike. Her favorite holiday is the one that is coming up next!